WALKS AROUND

C000001149

Settle &
Malham

10 WALKS 6 MILES OR LESS

Dalesman

Dalesman Publishing Company Ltd
Stable Courtyard, Broughton Hall,
Skipton, North Yorkshire BD23 3AZ
www.dalesman.co.uk

First Edition 1999, Reprinted 2003

Text © Richard Musgrave

Illustrations © Christine Isherwood:
p7 Janet's Foss, p8 hares, p11 grey wagtails, p13 bird's eye primrose,
p20 redshank, p23 green woodpecker, p27 packhorse bridge,
Stainforth, p30 globe flower, wood cranesbill and water avens

Maps by Jeremy Ashcroft

Cover : Malham Cove by Keith Watson

A British Library Cataloguing in Publication record
is available for this book

ISBN 1 85568 161 7

Printed by Amadeus Press, Cleckheaton

Contents

Introduction

Malham and Settle are almost neighbours geographically; however, when it comes to character and appearance, they differ enormously.

Settle is a busy market town with an abundance of amenities and a famous railway passing through. Malham is an ancient Dales village, which thrives on tourism. However, the two have one thing in common— limestone. Both centres are encompassed with spectacular limestone scenery. Additionally, both locations offer easily accessible, natural attractions, many of which are visited during the following walks.

Happy walking.

Richard Musgrave, January 1999

Recommended maps to aid navigation:

OS Outdoor Leisure Map 10 - Yorkshire Dales Southern Area
Stile Maps - Malhamdale
Transport - Pennine Motor Services

Janet's Foss (Gordale Scar optional) and the Cove

Length of Walk: 3½ miles + 1 mile Gordale Scar optional
Start: Malham
Terrain: Easy. 400 plus steps to descend from Cove!

Set off from the main car park walking towards Malham village as far as Sparth House Hotel. At that point cross the road and the footbridge over Malham Beck and turn right. On reaching a double set of gates (indicative of the heavy pedestrianisation!) swing left following the sign to Janet's Foss.

The route continues alongside Gordale Beck, eventually entering the National Trust woodland (lots of birds and wildflowers in season) enroute to Janet's Foss, a superb waterfall where sheep used to be washed in the pool below. Janet, according to legend, was a fairy queen who lived in a cave close to the waterfall.

Follow the path to the left of the waterfall, then turn right to walk along a road for about 100 yards seeking a signpost on the left to Malham Cove. Those wishing to visit Gordale Scar should continue along the road a short distance to a waymarked gate. After seeing Gordale Scar and its attractions return to the Malham Cove signpost.

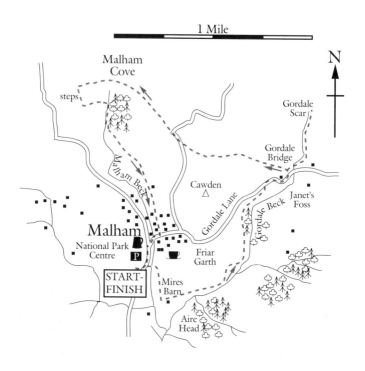

The clear path rises towards a ladder stile, then continues to a gate — turn left. The route is obvious and emerges at a road, where wonderful views of Malhamdale are presented.

Cross the road using the adjacent stiles, and then continue along a pleasant green swathe, seeking a signpost to Malham Cove, on the left. A superb view of the Cove appears at that point.

Hop over the ladder stile and explore the features of Malham's Cove — clints and grykes in abundance. Don't go near the edge!

After crossing the vast limestone area, descend the 400 plus steps. At the bottom of the steps turn left, and left again where paths merge to walk towards the Cove itself. Malham Beck has to be forded at this point —

you'll see the exit stiles across the water. (If the beck proves impassable return to the foot of the steps and turn left to follow the main track to Malham village.)

Once over the water follow the beck downstream for 150 yards towards a gate. Pass through, then swing slightly left, rising between two hawthorn trees. Proceed towards a gate with a stile alongside, then follow an obvious path into Malham, emerging alongside The Listers Arms. Turn right, cross the bridge; turn left for the car park.

Micklaw Hill

Length of Walk: 3¹/₂ miles
Start: Malham
Terrain: Moderate. Uphill from Malham to Micklaw Hill

Only three and a half miles in distance, but this outing lacks nothing when it comes to enjoyment and varied terrain. The ascent out of Malham offers sensational views, while the concluding section passes the spot where the infant River Aire re-emerges from the limestone depths, a location known as Aire Head.

Set out from the national park centre car park; turn right immediately to enter a lane. Continue straight on, ignoring the Pikedaw indicator.

The lane gradually rises and reaching a point when it levels out two landmarks appear on the right: the unmistakable Pikedaw Hill with the pointed cairn prominent. At a lower level are examples of strip lynchets, the ancient,

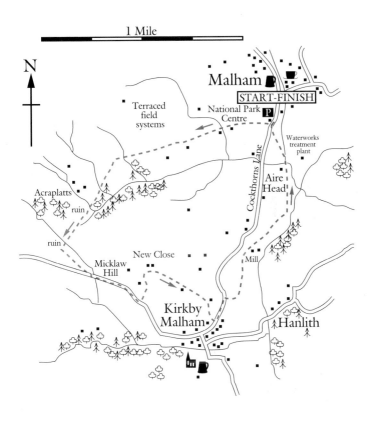

terraced field systems fashioned by early settlers centuries ago.

Follow the lane to its conclusion where a stile gives access into the field. Now the hard work starts! A signpost points the direction towards a ladder stile, which soon appears and is a superb viewpoint.

Continue towards a second ladder stile, resting close to the large barn, then following the wall to your left, rise to another ladder stile. Cross this, turn left and accompany the boundary wall to reach yet another stile. The farm on the right (to be ignored) is Acraplatts Farm.

Cross the field, heading diagonally left, and locate a footbridge (out of sight) in a depression. Once over the bridge walk uphill passing to the left of a ruin and locate a stile in the facing wall. Now head towards the horizon seeking a stile set amid the ruins of Old Acraplatts farm.

Turn left along the access road and enjoy the rewards of your physical efforts! It's all downhill from here; Micklaw Hill the high point.

Merging with the road turn left, then after 400 yards swing left into a farm access road signposted Cockthorns Lane. After passing the house on the left, proceed through a gate, (a tourist board indicator affixed), and turn right immediately crossing a grassed area towards a ladder stile.

Hop over the stile then gradually curve to the right, making towards a gate. After this keep the wall on the left in contention and walk to the bottom of the field where a gate leads out into Cockthorns Lane — turn right.

At the main road veer left to a signpost — Malham, then cross the field aiming for a stile in the wall, situated to the right of a large tree. The hamlet of Hanlith will be in view on the right.

A clear path crosses the next field, gradually descending towards Scalegill Mill — see notice board. Follow the narrow path to the left of the mill buildings and on to Malham. Along the way seek out Aire Heads, where the River Aire re-emerges from its subterranean world. This point is located about 100 yards before encountering a small waterworks installation.

Kirkby Malham

Length of Walk: 3 miles
Start: Kirkby Malham
Terrain: Easy. Fields and Riverside

Unlike many neighbouring villages whose suffixes 'ton' and 'ham' indicate Anglo-Saxon origins (sixth and seventh centuries), Kirkby Malham is a Scandinavian settlement (tenth century). The present church was erected during the 15th century replacing a much older building.

The visitors' book contains two signatures of Oliver Cromwell, dated 1665. A copy is available for inspection.

There's a small parking area at the eastern end of the bridge, diagonally adjacent to the public house. From that spot head towards the church, seeking a signpost (Otterburn) on the left, at the far end of the church's car park.

Cross the footbridge, climb the steps to a gate,

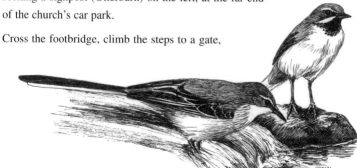

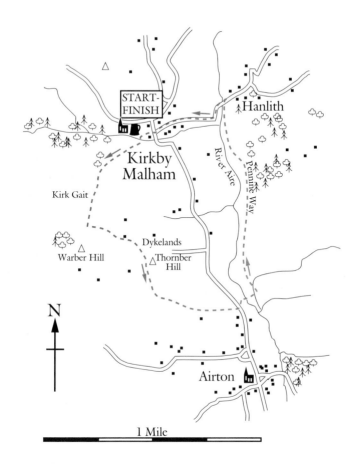

N

1 Mile

then continue curving slightly right towards a gap stile in the facing wall. Maintain the uphill course to another stile, and then aim for the copse of trees resting at the top of the hill.

Now head across the open pasture, following the line dictated by the waymarker — diagonally left. Head towards the far corner of the field, using a footbridge to cross a stream running in a depression. Beyond this locate a stile in the wall, situated to the right of a gate.

Continue walking with the wall on your left, then turn left through a gateway — signposted Airton. Head across the field, gradually descending towards a gate resting in the bottom left-hand corner of the field, close to a large barn.

Leave the field, seeking a stile directly opposite the barn. Cross the next field seeking a stile in the left-hand corner — ignore the wide gate.

Two additional stiles are navigated, then veer left seeking another stile almost concealed in a wall angle. Turn left to follow a cart track through a gateway, then continue through the gate directly ahead, and follow the wall to your right towards the main road. A signpost indicating Warber Hill in the opposite direction confirms the exact location.

Turn right and walk along the road for 20 yards then turn left —signposted Malham. Descend to the River (Aire), cross the footbridge and turn left following the Pennine Way footpath as far as Hanlith Bridge. At the bridge swing left, and follow the lane for half a mile to Kirkby Malham.

Around Airton

> **Length of Walk: 2¹/₂ miles**
> **Start: Airton**
> **Terrain: Easy. Fields and riverside. Soft going section!**

Airton is an Anglo-Saxon settlement — the town by the Air(e). The village has a large green area, a mill which once produced Dettol and now offers comfortable residential accommodation, and a Friends Meeting House.

Embark on this short but enjoyable ramble from the village green, striding along the road towards Otterburn and Hellifield. Ignore the turning to Bell Busk, instead continue along the road seeking a large barn on the left, known as Tormire Laithe. There's a signpost to Kirk Syke.

Cross the field to a ladder stile, then maintain the same course towards another stile. Go half-left, making towards a barn, and join the farm access road. Pass to the right of the barn and on to a wide gate giving access to the farmyard.

There are plenty of waymarkers to assist navigation through the farm. The easy way from the gate is left, right, left! Arriving at a junction swing right, descending along an uneven track. After passing a barn, and before reaching another, swing left through a stile.

Head across the field to a gateway, situated to the right of a large tree. Beyond the gateway veer slightly right, aiming for the bottom corner of a tree plantation. Hereabouts the terrain often has the consistency of treacle!

Make towards a gate that leads onto a road and turn left. At the junction turn right towards Gargrave, noting the old telephone exchange building. Cross Newfield Bridge, then pass through the stile on the left to follow the Pennine Way route alongside the infant River Aire. Watch out for kingfishers and dippers along the way.

The route crosses several stiles, but problems shouldn't arise, emerging at Airton Bridge with the converted mill close by. Turn left, and cross the bridge to re-enter Airton village, noting the Friends Meeting House on the left and a cottage opposite, bearing a datestone of 1696 and the initials E W A. These represented William and Alice Ellis who were Quakers themselves.

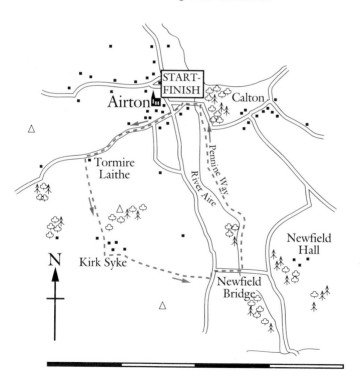

Weets Top

Length of Walk: 6 miles
Start: Malham
Terrain: Steep incline along Hawthorns Lane
* Not to be undertaken when misty conditions prevail

A full six-mile expedition, which visits Janet's Foss and the ancient monastic boundary marker — the Weets Cross (only the base remains).

Set out from the main car park situated alongside the national park centre. Turn left to walk towards the village centre. Reaching the Sparth House Hotel cross the road and the 'clapper' bridge across Malham Beck.

Now swing right and follow the indicators towards Janet's Foss. The route is reasonably straightforward, but make sure to turn left at the first set of double gates (signpost) and pass Mires Barn.

The route continues alongside Gordale Beck, and enters a woodland which is delightfully decorated with wildflowers in season, before arriving at the waterfall (see notice board).

Climb the rocky path to the left of the waterfall, then turn right to walk along the road. After passing a farmhouse the road (Hawthorns Lane) rises steeply, but offers superb retrospective views as it does. The road also runs adjacent to the line of the Mid Craven Fault — a geological point of interest.

After climbing out of the valley enter a lane on the right — signposted Weets

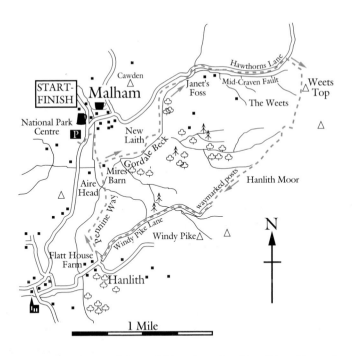

Top, and complete the remaining uphill section. Reaching Weets Top and the cross, past geological upheaval is graphically illustrated. The hill on which the cross stands consists of black gritstone — note the walling materials. Barely a mile away looking towards Gordale, everything is white limestone. The division caused by the forces of nature thousands of years ago is obvious.

The long descent to Hanlith gets underway after passing through the gate initially following the indication to Calton. After ten minutes walking, veer right at a signpost to Hanlith. Cross the stile then follow the marker poles across Hanlith Moor to arrive at a gate and access into Windy Pike Lane. Scintillating views hereabouts.

The uneven lane eventually gives way to a metalled surface and twists and turns to arrive at Flatt House Farm. Leave the road just before the farmhouse on the right to pass through a waymarked gate and follow the Pennine Way route into Malham which comes into view within a few minutes.

Otterburn Moor

Length of Walk: 5 miles
Start: Otterburn
Terrain: Rolling, exposed pastureland

Otterburn is a tidy, reclusive village resting about three miles east of Hellifield. The village has no amenities — hence the lack of visitors, but it is a picturesque spot and worthy of further inspection.

Set out from the bridge, walking alongside Otterburn Beck, heading in the opposite direction to Bell Busk - there's a signpost to Kirkby Malham. Pass through the confines of Grove Farm and follow an uneven track running alongside the beck until confronted by two gates. At this point continue straight on (forsaking the Kirkby Malham route) maintaining the beckside route, eventually passing Park House and High Barn.

Soon after this location the track rises and peters out. At that point veer slightly right away from the beck, and head across the large, open pasture making towards a wide gate in the facing wall. Pass through the gate then following the wall to your right make towards another gate situated in the top right hand corner of the field.

Enter a wide track known as Orms Gill Lane and turn left. Follow the lane beyond Orms Gill Green Farm (note the gigantic kiln), seeking a gate on the left immediately beyond where the stone wall ends.

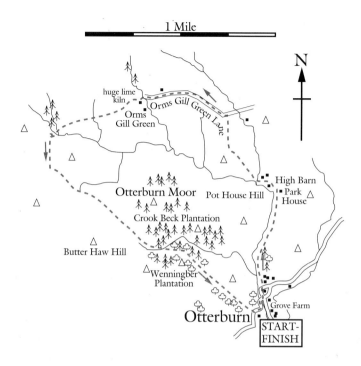

N

huge lime
kiln

Orms
Gill Green

Orms Gill Green Lane

Otterburn Moor

Pot House Hill

High Barn
Park
House

Crook Beck Plantation

Butter Haw Hill

Wenningber
Plantation

Otterburn

Grove Farm

START-
FINISH

*The next mile towards Langber Lane needs careful navigation, although the
line to be followed is almost straight and only two enclosures are crossed to
the next signpost.*

Pass through the gate and follow an obvious path for a few paces to reach
the top of a slight banking. Maintain the previous line, across the field
towards a stile in the facing wall. The stile comprises a tiny gate, set
between upright posts.

Follow the same course across a depression and a large, open pasture to
arrive at a four-way signpost erected at a rather remote location, to the left
of a copse of beech trees.

From the signpost head towards Langber Lane, which entails following the wall to your left. Reaching the lane turn left — signposted Otterburn. The route back to Otterburn follows an almost straight line and problems shouldn't arise.

After passing through three intervening gates the route descends to another gate giving access to woodland. Superb views are presented at the second gate. Butter Haw Hill with Pendle Hill in the background, are both on the right.

Following an obvious track the way continues along Dacre Lane to merge with a main road. Turn left into Otterburn.

Short, Steep, Spectacular Settle!

Length of Walk: 3 miles
Start: Settle
Terrain: Uphill out. Downhill in

This ramble is a short, yet pleasant introduction to the Settle area. The outward leg presents a rewarding physical challenge. The homeward section displays far-reaching views, which extend to the Cumbrian fells. Save this outing for a clear day.

Set off from the centre of Settle, passing to the right of the Shambles, then the TSB bank. Keep right of the estate agency to enter Chapel Square and on to Greenfoot car park. Veer left at the telephone box and right when the path forks to follow the path beyond the bungalows and on to the main road. Turn right, cross the road and enter Brockholes Lane on the left — a badly eroded signpost indicates Meer Beck.

Note the terraced field systems beyond the allotments on the left, before meeting up with Meer Beck, which covers the lane particularly after prolonged rainfall.

Leave the lane at a stile on the left when a signpost to Lodge is reached close

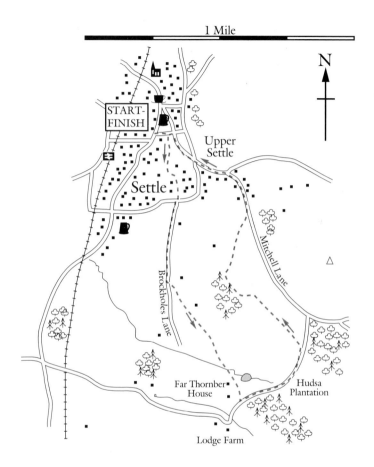

to a gate. The climb starts here! After 50 yards veer left to follow a faint green track, rising between two copses and on towards a narrow stile in the facing wall.

Proceed beyond a plantation, pass through an open gate and turn right to walk between a row of hawthorn trees and a wall towards a house and a stile.

Pass to the left of the house then swing left at a junction before reaching Lodge Farm to rise alongside Hudsa plantation, where the rewards for your physical efforts commence.

Leaving the plantation behind, continue to the end of the enclosed section, pass through the gate, swing immediately left to cross the ladder stile (the signpost to Turnpike House isn't relevant) and swing right heading towards Settle.

Walk across the rough pasture with the wall to your right, the views improving with every stride. As the wall descends, locate a stile 20 yards before reaching a wooded area. Cross the next field gradually curving left to a small gate, then turn right towards Mitchell Lane.

Reaching that point swing left to return to the centre of Settle. The field systems observed earlier are again conspicuous on the left.

Victoria Cave and Warrendale Knotts

Length of Walk: 4 miles
Start: Settle
Terrain: Uphill departure from Settle

Victoria Cave was rediscovered in May 1838, by a group of young men hunting foxes with terriers. Soon after, the cave was found to contain huge stalactites and evidence from the interglacial period: things like straight tusked elephant and slender nosed rhinoceros, woolly hippopotamus, oxen and even remains of hyena.

Set out at the north east corner of the Market Square, passing to the left of the Shambles, to enter Constitution Hill. A short way beyond Town Head Cottage enter a stony track on the right, rising steeply towards the limestone hills. Note the reference to a 'Mad Bull' on the right!

At the top of the rise pass through the gate and continue ahead, ignoring the right turn to Malham. Pass through another gate and enter an enclosed lane where superb views of Ribblesdale are evident. Pen-y-ghent appears directly ahead. Ignore a ladder stile on the left; instead continue through another gate, veer right towards limestone outcrops to follow a green path to pass beneath two copses.

Merging with the road swing right, following a secondary road that skirts around the perimeter of the copse. Follow this road beyond a barn (signpost Victoria Cave) to pass through a wide gate and turn right towards the cave.

Cross a ladder stile and proceed straight on, making a slight detour left to visit Victoria Cave after 200 yards. After seeing the huge cave continue in the previous direction, eventually descending along a bumpy path.

Midway down the uneven track cross a ladder stile, then continue downwards, turning right at the bottom. Locate a signpost resting beneath the imposing limestone outcrops — Warrendale Knotts, and follow the indication to Settle. Cross a ladder stile hidden in the left angle of the enclosure and rise along a pleasant green swathe.

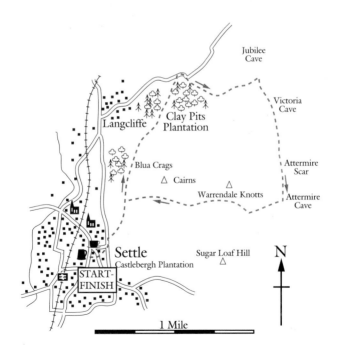

At a junction veer left (there's a tempting cave to the right!) then when the path begins to descend take in the vista. The flat-topped Ingleborough stands majestically to the right; straight ahead the chasm of Giggleswick Scar quarry is unmistakeable. Beyond the quarry, on the right are the lakeland fells. On the left the dome shaped outline of the Scottish hills.

Now just follow the clear track downhill (ignoring the right turn) to rejoin the path used on the outward route to return to Settle.

The Hoffman Kiln and the Ribble Valley

Length of Walk: 4 miles
Start: Langcliffe
Terrain: Easy throughout

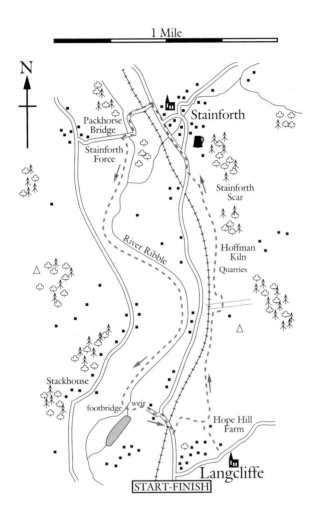

Langcliffe is a pleasant village, hiding only yards from the B6479 road, a couple of miles north of Settle. The village has retained its school and post office, and has a large car parking area across the road from the impressive church of St John the Evangelist.

The walk sets out from the car park following the indication of the signpost. Entering a lane swing right at Hope Hill Farm and continue for 200 yards to hop over a stile towards Stainforth (signpost).

Walking along a clear path cross a succession of stiles to emerge at a road. Cross straight over to walk alongside the famous Settle-Carlisle railway, soon entering a disused depot. Swing left towards the first point of interest — the gigantic Hoffman Kiln, used in the production of slake lime during the first half of the 20th century.

The walk continues alongside the kiln, crosses a tiny bridge, then rises to a stile and follows a clear path across the fields gradually edging towards the road where a stile is situated. Turn right along the road towards Stainforth. If wishing to visit Stainforth bear right at the junction, otherwise follow the main road. Beyond the Old School House on the left turn into a narrow road and descend to Stainforth Packhorse Bridge, built in 1670 by a Quaker named Samuel Watson. Stainforth's name is derived from stony-ford.

At the far end of the bridge turn left through the stile to follow the riverside route towards Stackhouse. Note the spectacular waterfalls, Stainforth Force, where salmon leap in season. Also, be aware that the route departs from the river briefly, about 200 yards beyond the caravan park seen on the right.

Approaching Stackhouse recross the Ribble at the footbridge near the weir, turn left and rise to the main road. Cross over veering right to enter a lane signposted Pike Lane. After 50 yards turn right through a waymarked gate and accompany the wall on the left to a small gate situated at the top of the field. Enter the lane and turn right to Langcliffe.

Catrigg Force and Stainforth Scar

Length of Walk: 3¹/₂ miles
Start: Stainforth (car park)
Terrain: Uphill to Catrigg Force

Cowside Beck, which gathers momentum across Malham Moor, crashes in spectacular fashion through a narrow passage to the east of Stainforth. This is Catrigg Force, a high waterfall visited long ago by the great composer Edward Elgar. The Force is the feature of this short but satisfying outing.

Leave the car park (alongside the B6479 road) at Stainforth, walking past the telephone box towards the village centre. At the road junction turn right; cross the bridge then immediately pass through a stile on the left to walk alongside Stainforth Beck.

Merging with a road turn left, pass 'the green' then turn right and commence the upward slog to the waterfall.

At the top of the lane turn left (signpost Catrigg Force) to visit the waterfall. Resume the walk from the other

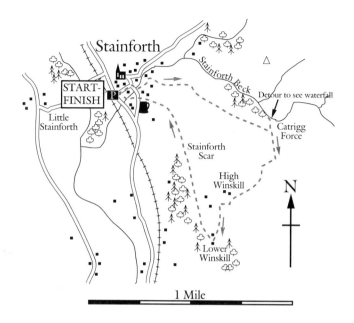

ladder stile, to walk along a vehicle track, which rises steadily towards another gate.

This spot is a wonderful location — the three highest points in Yorkshire are all in view! Ingleborough (left), Pen-y-ghent (right) the highest and least impressive, Whernside (centre).

The signpost points to Winskill, a location reached by following the track used previously. High Winskill is encountered first.

Pass through an open gateway to cross a stile situated alongside a facing gate and follow the signpost to Stainforth. This leads along the access road to Low Winskill farm. Pass between the buildings, cross a ladder stile and rise up the bank to follow a clear path. After 20 paces Stainforth appears far below.

After crossing two intervening ladder stiles the way enters a woodland and descends a limestone stairway (take care!) emerging into a field. Here turn right and follow the yellow painted markers towards Stainforth. Please fasten all gates.

Once in the village head towards the public house, cross the bridge and turn left to the car park.

Publisher's Note
The information given in this book has been provided in good faith and is intended only as a general guide. Whilst all reasonable efforts have been made to ensure that details were correct at the time of publication, the author and Dalesman Publishing Company Ltd cannot accept any responsibility for inaccuracies. It is the responsibility of individuals undertaking outdoor activities to approach the activity with caution and, especially if inexperienced, to do so under appropriate supervision. They should also carry the appropriate equipment and maps, be properly clothed and have adequate footwear. The sport described in this book is strenuous and individuals should ensure that they are suitably fit before embarking upon it.